Tomatoes for Shade

While every precaution has been taken in the preparation of this book, the publisher assumes no responsibility for errors or omissions, or for damages resulting from the use of the information contained herein.

TOMATOES FOR SHADE

FIRST EDITION. FEBRUARY 11, 2023.

Cover art – Daniel Keleman, based on [1].

Table of Contents

Dedicated to my grandmother.

Introduction

I've got a clear and intense memory from a couple of decades ago: I am about 6 years old, back in Transylvania, in the village of my grandparents. On a sunny morning, I am seeking ways to the backyard where they had an apiary, and they were also growing all sorts of vegetables and fruits. In this memory I finally find my path, I tear off a huge ripen tomato, and my nearly infinite joyride starts as I push my face into it. It smells so delicious as nothing else; I feel like in paradise and I chew that delicious thing until I finish. Without a thought, then I am already craving the next one. But a couple of minutes later, the idyllic moment dissipates as the bees begin to wake up and start their daily routine. The situation is getting hotter and hotter: thousands of little flying animals want to catch just me, so I realize it's time to go back to my grandparents' house.

Probably this short, dream-like memory is my first anchor to tomatoes! The summer vibes, the taste and the smell of that tomato, and the idea of how I secretly embraced it, all led me to the recognition that I want to revive that moment. I must admit that the straightest way to do that is to plant and grow tomatoes in whatever circumstances. Now I am in the present again, and it happened; for years repeatedly, and I do it with greater and greater success and joy. By the way, did you know that in Hungarian, we call the tomato and paradise with the same exact word: paradicsom (IPA: /ˈpɒrɒditʃom/). What a coincidence, and how well they fit! In fact, the Hungarian word tomato is abbreviated from the phrase "apple of the paradise ". The plant's "apple" name is still preserved by its Italian name (pomodoro, i.e. "golden apple"). Tomato in Spanish is tomate, a word of Aztec origin: the Spanish conquistadors abbreviated the original Aztec name xitomatl of the fruit brought from America. This word then entered many European languages: for example French and German tomate, English tomato.

The circumstances of the present? They are great, but not so great as they were at that time: in contrast to the huge fields of the Transylvanian countryside, we live now next to Budapest, the capital of Hungary. This area is more densely populated, and our garden is tinier and shadier. However, I figured out how to grow tomatoes in this new environment and I also found the types of tomatoes that are OK with the shadows.

And this is the reason I wrote this little book... to motivate you by sharing my experiences and maybe providing a bit of guidance. To show you that even in not the most optimal parameters, tomatoes can be grown. My goal is not to cover all the aspects of tomato growing, so many tried that already and there is great literature, and I will recommend some of the bests of that at the end of this book. The goal of this book is:

(1) to motivate you growing tomatoes in a suboptimal (shady) environment,
(2) to provide hacks to grow tomatoes in shady and little places, and
(3) to recommend the best tomatoes to grow in shade.

This book is definitely for tomato lovers who do not have the best environment, but still want to try tomato growing and want to have success (in the shadows)!

Should You Give it a Try?

You can still enjoy the pleasures of gardening and growing tomatoes even if you have a small and shady space. This is exactly what I do for five years now.

Years ago, we moved into a village next to Budapest, Hungary to a small house with a tiny garden. The whole area is rather shady, it's just about a couple of square meters and we got huge Leyland trees and neighboring houses very close. The whole plot is 300 square meters, but it includes the house, a garage, a garden storage, a terrace, a paved area for a car, so all in all, the garden itself is just less than 100 square meters. In this little, tiny place we planted so many fruits and vegetables, that it's hard to believe it. We got an apple tree, a cherry tree, a fig tree, vines, dogwood, blackberries, Kamchatka honey berries, white currants, black currants, red currants, strawberries, raspberries, a jostaberries, gooseberries, blueberries. And then each year we plant several vegetables as well, including tomatoes (about 30 seedlings, around 10 varieties per year). To go even further, one of my friends lives in a 40 square meters apartment together with his wife. The apartment has no terrace, but only a shady hanging corridor. They plant all sort of herbs, spices, and tomatoes every year on that corridor. If they can, I can, and you can! Even if you have a small garden or just a terrace you can plant and grow so many things, and one best option, I can tell you after five years of great experience is planting and growing tomatoes.

Plus, no one requires you to start big, you can start with one single plant, for which you need one single seed (OK, for safety reasons maybe two or three). With baby steps you can find out if this is your thing. You will realize that even the very small and early steps are an amazing adventure!

Benefits of Planting Tomatoes

The answer from benefits side is pretty simple, I can formulate it with just three words: Relax, joy and fun.

The relaxation part comes when you start gathering the things needed for planting. In Hungary it starts early in the year, around the beginning of February. You plant the seeds and when they are grown, you put them outdoors into the garden or to a terrace or anywhere they can get water and some sunlight. The relaxation in it is that you do something completely different from what you are used to, something else what you do at work. The good thing is that when you start cultivating your plants you can forget everything else and do all caring activities with your plants. It ends only around October when you have the latest ripening. Caring about anything, even just about a plant is really a relaxing activity!

The fun is when tomatoes start cropping and you and probably also the members of your family can't wait to have the end-result. When you see day by day how your plants and tomatoes are growing is a fun and nice feeling. If you have kids, it will be so much fun to water them together and if they also addicted to them, it is also fun to keep them away till the tomatoes are fully cropped.

The joy comes when you taste your own grown tomatoes. Then you can just go and pick one and eat it as is or make a tasty salad or use it in so many ways. You will enjoy the end-result of your work which lasted for multiple months. You will realize the taste difference between your own tomatoes and the ones you can buy in a random supermarket. The difference will be so huge, that you then can't wait to start over and over again!

Benefits of Shade

Don't forget that shade and little space have their benefits too. In the times of global warming, summers get hotter and hotter. Contrary to what many think, tomatoes are not heat lovers [2]. Shading vegetables including tomatoes is not an uncommon thing of gardeners in hotter climates (for instance in southern parts of Europe and southern U.S.) [3]. Providing shade is a helpful way to keep plants producing during the summer heat or at least help reduce their stress. When the temperature gets hot during the day (over 30C/85F) or are too hot overnight (over 30C/70F) many plants, especially vegetables including tomatoes will drop their blossoms. Thus, decreased exposure to the direct sunlight can have its benefits e.g., a decreasing the risk of dehydration and stress.

Drawback of the Shade

As we discussed previously, most of the tomatoes need 8 hours of direct sun every day to produce the best results, but they can tolerate partial shade. Grown in shade will often result in more leggy plants that are looking for extra sunlight; these tomatoes will have a smaller fruit set and take longer to ripen. Therefore, the best results come from growing smaller varieties like cherry tomatoes, but in partial shade this is also achievable with larger tomato varieties. It's important to keep other factors like water, nutrients, and air flow as optimal as you can if growing tomatoes in shade, so they reach their potential health wise and yield wise [4].

Although many tomato cultivars are suitable for shadow gardens, gardeners frequently report lower yields. More plants can be cultivated to help get around this problem. Growing tomatoes in the shade might also result in higher disease rates. Tomato plants' air circulation is increased through trellising and pruning [5].

Hacking the Shade

I am not going to lie, tomatoes love sunshine. Plus, the tomato plants need space. Obviously both statements contradict the mission of this book. Nevertheless, how can you grow tomatoes in a small and shady place? Let's see the simplest options.

The usual sunlight needed for a tomato is about 8 hours per day. Sunlight is converted into energy through the process of photosynthesis. During photosynthesis, the tomatoes absorb energy from the sun and use it to combine carbon dioxide and water to form sugar, or glucose. This sugar is then used as energy for the plant's growth and development.

Have you got a shady place? You most probably won't have 8 hours a day light, therefore are here, right? The good news is that all wannabe tomato growers are lucky because the tomato is a rapidly growing crop! The usual growing period is 90 to 150 days. It means if you select the tomato types carefully, you perform the process right and you got plenty of sunshine, then in 3-4 months you can get the tomatoes.

But how can you hack the 8 hours need of sunlight? Well, you can play with other parameters, such as:

- Choosing tomatoes which have very short growing period. Yes, it can grow in a way shorter period of time than 90 days, we will see those varieties later. I will present tomatoes that need only around 50-60 days, what a difference! Due to the shorter growing period, your tomatoes still might not get the 8 hours sunshine per day, but they will have extended timeframe to grow compared to their recommended number of days.

- Choosing different places that you imagined at first. Everyone has windows where we live. Would it be possible to grow tomatoes in near the window? The answer is probably yes, then you just need to do the container growing right and choose the tomato seeds or later plans carefully. Dwarf tomatoes could also do a great job in this aspect!

Getting the Seeds

Now you already know I am mad about tomatoes. It's just crazy how addicted I become year by year for planting and growing these wonderful vegetables. (Botanically speaking tomatoes are fruits, because they contain seeds and grow from the flower of the tomato plant, however tomatoes are typically prepared in tasty dishes, which is why they are usually referred as a vegetable from a culinary perspective [6], [7]). Back to getting the seeds: as a first step, you can start with seeds from the supermarkets, that's an easy way to start. As a second option you can go the gardening shops, you will find plenty of types to start (e.g. you will surely find Sand Marzano or Black Cherry in generic shops). However, in case if you are really looking for specific types you should look at tomato seed sites. Pomidorlandia [8], Totally Tomatoes [9], Jung Seeds [10], Baker Creek [11] or T&T Seeds [12] are good starting points among many others.

Finally, the solution I usually chose is local gardening online forums. The huge benefit of such forums that you can ask questions and gain experiences of others before purchasing any seeds. Additionally, it is also quite common that experts are selling a huge variety of seeds for a fraction of price of the well-known brands. One great forum I am purchasing tomatoes from is the Hungarian Tomato Growers Facebook group [13], where many sell ~20 seeds for just as little as ~$1 . Often these local sellers have dozens or hundreds of rare types. One drawback of purchasing from online forums is that the pollination might not be assured as precisely as at official seed producers, but that is often mentioned and not a huge risk in my experience.

Tomatoes for Shade

San Marzano

Main parameters
Fruit Color: **Bright Red;** Germination: **7 to 21;** Maturity: **80;**
Determinate or indeterminate: **Indeterminate;**
Hybrid / Open Pollinated: **Open Pollinated**

Description

This is the number one tomato everyone should plant. It has such a heritage, it has got an immense history, and most importantly: multiple varieties of San Marzano can be successfully grown in shady, little places. It is not just my recommendation, but also the number one tomato the seeds dealer from I got most of my seeds offers for shady gardens.

San Marzano tomatoes have a long history of being a favorite among Italian cooks. The tomato variety is native to the area around Mount Vesuvius and San Marzano sul Sarno in Campania, Italy, and has been cultivated for centuries for its unique flavor and texture.

The San Marzano variety is believed to be descended from the original pomodoro di oro – or "golden apple" – tomatoes originally brought to Italy from the Americas in the 16th century. They are an heirloom variety of tomato characterized by their thin, elongated shape and bright red color. This variety is sought after due to its distinct taste, which has been said to be sweeter and less acidic than other tomato varieties.

These tomatoes are also known for their higher sugar content as well as their high concentration of lycopene, a powerful antioxidant that can help protect against cancer and heart disease. In fact, according to recent studies, they contain up to three times more lycopene than regular tomatoes – making them an even healthier choice!

San Marzanos are also rich in vitamins A and C, potassium, folate, iron, magnesium and calcium – all important nutrients for overall health and wellness. Additionally, these tomatoes can be used in many different recipes ranging from sauces to salads and much more. Due to their popularity with chefs around the world, San Marzano tomatoes have become one of the most widely grown varieties of tomatoes in Italy. In fact, many people claim that authentic Italian pizzerias won't even use any other type of tomato on their pizzas! [14]

When buying San Marzano tomatoes, it's important to look for ones that are labeled DOP (Protected Designation of Origin). This means that they were grown within the confines set out by Italian law; without this label you may not be getting an authentic product. Additionally look for cans or jars labeled "Presa Extra" or "Pomodori Pelati", both of which imply superior quality due to specific processing methods employed during production.

Overall San Marzano tomatoes are an excellent addition to any recipe thanks to their sweet flavor profile as well as their numerous health benefits. Whether you're looking for a delicious pizza topping or just looking for something with more nutrients than traditional grocery store varieties offer - you simply cannot go wrong with this beloved heirloom tomato variety!

Redorta

Main parameters
Fruit Color: **Red**; Germination: **7 to 21**; Maturity: **78**;
Determinate or indeterminate: **Indeterminate**;
Hybrid / Open Pollinated: **Open Pollinated**

Description
Named for a mountain, Pizzo Redorta in Bergamo, Italy, with much better taste than its cousin, San Marzano. Redorta is a tomato cultivar recognized for its unusual form and rich flavor. Redorta tomatoes are medium-sized, round and somewhat flattened tomatoes with slightly meaty flesh and a sweet, slightly acidic flavor. Gardeners and home cooks love Redorta tomatoes for their flexibility in the kitchen, since they can be used in anything from salads and sandwiches to sauces and stews. They are especially popular among gardeners due to their very simple growth habits, which are minimal maintenance and disease-resistant.

Black Cherry

Main parameters
Fruit Color: **Black Cherry;** Germination: **7 to 21;** Maturity: **70;**
Determinate or indeterminate: **Indeterminate;**
Hybrid / Open Pollinated: **Open Pollinated**

Description
Black cherries tomatoes are more than just a stunningly dark, nearly black addition to any salad - they are a plant-lover's delight! Not only are they small, sweet and less acidic than other varieties, but they also offer unique resilience to pests and ailments. And, because of their sweet taste and handy size, these tomatoes make a delicious snack. The plants are determinate and usually only grow to about 3 feet tall, so even those with smaller spaces can enjoy the beauty, taste, and hardiness of the black cherry tomato.

Black cherry tomatoes are an excellent choice for gardeners looking to reap the health benefits of a nutritious vegetable. Not only do they have a good yield, producing large clusters of fruit, but they are also packed with essential vitamins and minerals. Rich in Vitamin C, Vitamin A, and Lycopene, these tomatoes are high in antioxidants which have anti-inflammatory properties and are low in calories. All of this makes them an excellent addition to any diet.

Evan's Purple

Main parameters
Fruit Color: **Purple;** Germination: **7 to 14;** Maturity: **75;**
Determinate or indeterminate: **Indeterminate;**
Hybrid / Open Pollinated: **Open Pollinated**

Description
The Evans Purple tomato is a rare and unique heirloom variety that has been passed down through generations. It is known for its deep purple color and sweet flavor, making it a popular choice among tomato growers. The tomatoes are typically small to medium in size and have a slightly flattened shape, giving them a rich and complex flavor with a balance of sweetness and acidity. The plants are indeterminate and can grow up to 8 feet tall, making them a little bit more challenging to grow than other tomato varieties. However, they are known to be disease resistant, making them a great choice for tomato growers looking for an unusual variety.

Pear Golden

Main parameters

Fruit Color: **Yellow;** Germination: **7 to 21;** Maturity: **78;**
Determinate or indeterminate: **Indeterminate;**
Hybrid / Open Pollinated: **Open Pollinated**

Description

The Pear Golden tomato is an exquisite variety of tomato that is renowned for its small, pear-shaped fruit and golden yellow coloring. Its sweet and juicy taste, with a low acidity, makes it a great choice for salads, eating fresh, or preserving due to its unique shape. The plants typically grow to about 3 feet tall and are known to be disease-resistant, producing a good yield. This variety of tomato is also considered to be a great option for container gardening. With its attractive and flavorful fruit, the Pear Golden tomato is sure to make a delightful addition to any garden.

Sweet Ildi

Main parameters

Fruit Color: **Yellow;** Germination: **7 to 21;** Maturity: **53;**
Determinate or indeterminate: **Indeterminate;**
Hybrid / Open Pollinated: **Open Pollinated**

Description

Sweet Ildi are yellow tomatoes. These are an heirloom variety with a unique flavor and color. Known for its small size and sweet taste, these tomatoes are a prized gourmet variety. They have a slightly flattened shape and range in size from small to medium. With a sweet and tangy taste, these tomatoes are excellent for salads and eating fresh. The plants are indeterminate and can grow up to 4-5 feet tall, although they can be more challenging to grow than other tomatoes. They are disease resistant and make a great addition to any garden!

The Sweet Ildi Yellow tomato is an early-season variety that matures and is ready to be harvested earlier than other tomato varieties. This determinate variety has a compact growth habit and produces large clusters of fruit with a good yield. It is also disease-resistant and tolerant to different weather conditions, making it a great option for home gardening and small scale commercial production. Sweet Ildi Yellow tomatoes are the perfect choice for fresh eating, salads, sandwiches, and cooking. Their versatility makes them a great addition to any kitchen.

Isis Candy Cherry

Main parameters

Fruit Color: **Yellow;** Germination: **7 to 21;** Maturity: **65;**
Determinate or indeterminate: **Indeterminate;**
Hybrid / Open Pollinated: **Open Pollinated**

Description

Also called as healthy sugar! Kids can't resist the sweet and fruity taste of these delicious tomatoes! These delightful, round one-inch fruits come in a range of colors from deep reds to golden yellows and often feature a unique "cat's eye" or star on the blossom end. Not only are they a hit with kids, but they can also add beauty and flavor to salads when you get them into the kitchen. With their irresistible taste, they hardly ever make it in the house - so get them while you can! A truly unique and delicious fruit, you won't want to miss out on! [15], [16]

Juliet Hybrid

Main parameters
Fruit Color: **Red;** Germination: **7 to 21;** Maturity: **60;**
Determinate or indeterminate: **Indeterminate;**
Hybrid / Open Pollinated: **Hybrid**

Description
It is well-known for producing the first elongated, grape-like fruits that do not crack! Clusters of unusual, sweet-flavored fruits cling to the vine for a longer period of time than most cherry tomatoes. Juliet Hybrid tomatoes are a type of hybrid tomato known for their high yields and disease resistance. It has a deep red color and is small to medium in size. Juliet tomatoes have smooth and firm skin, making them ideal for fresh eating as well as preserving and canning.

The plant produces an abundance of flavorful small to medium-sized fruit. It is also known for its disease resistance because it is less susceptible to common tomato diseases such as blossom end rot, cracking, and tomato mosaic virus. Also famous of leaf spot resistance.

The Juliet Hybrid tomato is frequently used in salads, sandwiches, and sauces. It's also a popular ingredient for making bruschetta, thanks to its sweet and juicy flavor.

Overall, the Juliet Hybrid tomato is a dependable and high-yielding variety suitable for both home gardens and commercial agriculture.

Its small size and disease resistance make it a popular choice among tomato growers.

Principe Borghese

Main parameters

Fruit Color: **Red**; Germination: **7 to 21**; Maturity: **70**;
Determinate or indeterminate: **Determinate**;
Hybrid / Open Pollinated: **Hybrid**

Description

The Italian heirloom known for sun drying. The grape-shaped fruit is very dry and has few seeds. It has a rich tomato flavor that is great for sauces. Vines produce an abundance of fruit clusters, which are ideal for selling in fresh markets and making specialty products. The Principe Borghese tomato is prized for its sweet and juicy flavor, as well as its high yield. It is a heavy producer, and it is not uncommon for a single plant to produce hundreds of small, cherry-sized tomatoes. The tomato has a bright red color and a firm, yet tender texture that makes it an ideal choice for drying, canning, or using in sauces.

In addition to its sweet and juicy flavor, the Principe Borghese tomato is also known for its versatility in the kitchen. It can be used in a variety of dishes, including salads, pasta sauces, and pizzas. It is also a popular choice for making sun-dried tomatoes, as its small size and high yield make it easy to preserve and enjoy throughout the year.

Overall, the Principe Borghese tomato is a high-yielding and flavorful variety that is well-suited to both home gardens and commercial agriculture. Its small size and sweet flavor make it a popular choice for preserving and using in a variety of recipes.

Vernissage Yellow

Main parameters
Fruit Color: **Yellow**; Germination: **7 to 21**; Maturity: **75**;
Determinate or indeterminate: **Indeterminate**;
Hybrid / Open Pollinated: **Hybrid**

Description
Vernissage tomatoes are large crops of Ukrainian tomatoes with beautiful foliage [17]. The Vernissage Yellow tomato is a hybrid variety of tomato that is prized for its unique yellow color and sweet, juicy flavor. It is a medium-sized tomato that ranges in shape from round to oblong, and it has a smooth, slightly-ridged skin.

One of the key features of the Vernissage Yellow tomato is its bright yellow color, which sets it apart from other tomato varieties. The yellow color is a result of a high concentration of carotenoids, which are compounds that give many fruits and vegetables their yellow and orange color.

In addition to its unique color, the Vernissage Yellow tomato is also known for its sweet, juicy flavor. It is a high-yielding variety that produces an abundance of medium-sized fruit that are packed with flavor. The tomato is also resistant to common tomato diseases, making it a popular choice among gardeners and farmers.

Mama Leone

Main parameters

Fruit Color: **Red**; Germination: **7 to 21**; Maturity: **75**;
Determinate or indeterminate: **Indeterminate;**
Hybrid / Open Pollinated: **Open Pollinated**

Description

A variety from Italy via a family who immigrated to New York, USA. These are the ideal tomatoes for making a rich tomato sauce in a simmering pot [18]. Long, fat tomatoes that turn red when ripe, seemingly these are smaller versions of Amish Paste. Mama Leone has a really pleasant aroma!

Roma

Main parameters
Fruit Color: **Red;** Germination: **7 to 21;** Maturity: **75;**
Determinate or indeterminate: **Determinate;**
Hybrid / Open Pollinated: **Open Pollinated**

Description
Roma is the most well-known paste-type tomato, ideal for sauces, pastes, and ketchup. Heavy crops of brilliant red, pear-shaped fruits with few seeds are delicious and meaty. They are a bright red color and have a firm flesh that is low in moisture and high in flavor.
Roma tomatoes are well-suited for cooking, as their meaty flesh makes them ideal for sauces, salsas, and pastes. They are also popular for drying, as their low moisture content means that they dry well and retain their flavor.

Arkansas Traveler

Main parameters
Fruit Color: **Red;** Germination: **7 to 21;** Maturity: **70 to 90;**
Determinate or indeterminate: **Indeterminate;**
Hybrid / Open Pollinated: **Open Pollinated**

Description
Developed at the University of Arkansas by Joe McFerran as a modern take on the renownedly superior pink tomatoes of the area. Arkansas Traveler is praised for its sweet and juicy flavor. It is a medium-sized tomato with a smooth, slightly ridged skin that ranges in hue from pink to pale red. Since the tomato continues to develop and bear fruit throughout the growing season, it is regarded as an indeterminate variety.

Because of its resilience to pests and diseases, the Arkansas Traveler tomato is a favorite with farmers and gardeners alike. The tomato is a good choice for growing in hot, humid settings because of its reputation for withstanding hard weather conditions. The Arkansas Traveler tomato is typically eaten fresh, and it is often used in salads and sandwiches. It is also a great ingredient for making sauces and soups, as it has a rich and sweet flavor that complements many different dishes. Overall, the Arkansas Traveler tomato is a versatile and flavorful variety that is a favorite among many gardeners and tomato enthusiasts.

Beauty

Main parameters

Fruit Color: **Pink;** Germination: **7 to 21;** Maturity: **85;**
Determinate or indeterminate: **Indeterminate;**
Hybrid / Open Pollinated: **Open Pollinated**

Description

Medium-sized, extremely prolific, leafy plant that produces a massive number of somewhat flattened fruits with enormous juicy, very sweet yet perfectly balanced with acid for rich, nuanced tomatoey tastes. One of my favorite tomatoes.

Belize Pink Heart

Main parameters
Fruit Color: **Pink;** Germination: **7 to 21;** Maturity: **75;**
Determinate or indeterminate: **Indeterminate;**
Hybrid / Open Pollinated: **Open Pollinated**

Description
This cultivar was discovered at a market in the town of Belize, as the name implies. A robust plant requires tying or staking. The meaty fruits are brilliantly pink with a very thin skin. They weigh around 300 grams on average [19].

Belize Pink Heart tomatoes are an heirloom tomato type notable for their enormous size, delicious meat, and heart-shaped appearance. They are often brilliant pink in color and have a sweet, somewhat acidic flavor that both home cooks and gardeners enjoy. Belize Pink Heart tomatoes have an indeterminate growth habit, which means they will continue to grow and produce fruit until the first hard frost. This makes them a popular choice for gardeners who wish to produce fresh tomatoes for a long time.

Belize Pink Heart tomatoes are also recognized for their disease resistance, making them a popular choice for gardeners looking to maintain healthy, productive plants without investing a lot of money.

Carmello

Main parameters

Fruit Color: **Pink**; Germination: **7 to 21**; Maturity: **70**;
Determinate or indeterminate: **Indeterminate**;
Hybrid / Open Pollinated: **Hybrid**

Description

Carmello has a taste that lasts for days! On sturdy, uniform plants, this excellent tomato produces big clusters of spherical fruit. For such an early hybrid tomato, its large fruit and well-developed taste are very noteworthy. It excels in every category: flavor, productivity, and endurance. The flavor is the pure essence of tomato, with a wonderful mix of sweet and acid. Indeterminate plants have a high level of disease resistance. It is immune to Verticillium Wilt and Fusarium Wilt [20], [21].

Early Wonder

Main parameters
Fruit Color: **Pale Pink**; Germination: **7 to 21**; Maturity: **54**;
Determinate or indeterminate: **Determinate**;
Hybrid / Open Pollinated: **Open Pollinated**

Description
This cultivar was introduced in 1950 by the Burgess Seed and Plant Co. Extra-early maturing and compact cultivar that produces an abundance of spherical, dark-pink, delicious fruit. Gardeners in short-season growing climates will love it. A fantastic choice for container gardening. Not too big in size, often extremely sweet.

Golden Sunray

Main parameters

Fruit Color: **Orange;** Germination: **7 to 21;** Maturity: **75-110;**

Determinate or indeterminate: **Indeterminate;**

Hybrid / Open Pollinated: **Hybrid**

Description

The Golden Sunray Tomato is a lovely orange-colored cultivar from the United States. The about 200 g brilliant orange, spherical tomatoes grow up to 2 metre tall plants. The fruit is fleshy and flavorful, with a sweet-sour balance. They are great for fresh consumption and offer a flavorful touch of color to salads, but they may also be cooked and used to make sauces.

Green Zebra

Main parameters
Fruit Color: **Green with stripes of light green**; Germination: **7 to 21**; Maturity: **78**;
Determinate or indeterminate: **Indeterminate;**
Hybrid / Open Pollinated: **Open Pollinated**

Description
Green Zebra is a tomato type praised for its distinct, green-striped look and acidic, sweet flavor. Green Zebra tomatoes range in size from medium to small and have a circular, somewhat flattened form. They have a juicy, tasty flesh that is acidic and slightly sweet, and they are green with yellow-green stripes.

Green Zebra tomatoes are ideal for fresh eating because of their acidic, sweet flavor and appealing, green-striped look, which makes them a standout in salads, sandwiches, and snacks. They're also popular in the kitchen, where their acidic flavor complements sauces, salsas, and other meals.

Green Zebra tomatoes have an indeterminate growth habit, which means plants will continue to grow and produce fruit until the first frost.

Marglobe

Main parameters

Fruit Color: **Red**; Germination: **7 to 21**; Maturity: **72**;
Determinate or indeterminate: **Determinate**;
Hybrid / Open Pollinated: **Open Pollinated**

Description

This versatile, flavorful old favorite gives a great output of globe-shaped fruits on uniform vines. Large fruits are also consistent, delicious, and thick-walled.

Marglobe tomatoes are well-suited for a variety of cooking applications, including sauces, stews, and salsas. They are also popular for canning and preserving, as their large size and firm flesh make them easy to handle and process.

Siberia

Main parameters
Fruit Color: **Red;** Germination: **7 to 21;** Maturity: **50;**
Determinate or indeterminate: **Determinate;**
Hybrid / Open Pollinated: **Open Pollinated**

Description

Siberia is a variety of tomato that is prized for its cold tolerance and ability to grow in cooler climates. Unlike many tomato varieties, which are heat-loving plants, Siberia tomatoes are able to withstand cooler temperatures and can be grown in regions with shorter growing seasons. This makes them a popular choice among gardeners who live in cooler climates and want to grow tomatoes without relying on heated greenhouses or other growing structures.

Because of its capacity to develop fruit in cold temperatures where other types will not, the prolific 'Siberia' tomato plants yield unusually early in the season. They're bright red and globe-shaped, weighing up to five ounces apiece.

'Siberia' was discovered for sale at a local nursery by Ron Driskill, a horticulture teacher at the Jack James Secondary School in Calgary, Alberta, Canada. The nurseryman informed him that in 1975, a woman visiting Canada from the Soviet Union went by the greenhouse and gave him 10 seedlings. The mysterious woman informed them that the variety was now being tested in Siberia.

Mr. Driskill saw its potential and became an outspoken booster of the variety among Northern gardeners, first by giving out seeds in return for money [22].

Tigerella

Main parameters
Fruit Color: **Red hue and yellow stripes;** Germination: **7 to 21;**
Maturity: **70;**
Determinate or indeterminate: **Indeterminate;**
Hybrid / Open Pollinated: **Open Pollinated**

Description
Tigerella, often known as "Tigre," is a tomato type praised for its unusual look and delectable flavor. Tigerella tomatoes are medium-sized, and spherical in form. They are distinguished by their vibrant red hue and yellow stripes, which give the fruit a striking tiger-like look, giving rise to the name "Tigerella."
Tigerella tomato flesh is firm and juicy, with a sweet and slightly tangy taste. They are ideal for fresh eating since their sweet and juicy flavor complements salads, sandwiches, and snacks. They're also popular in the kitchen, where their sweet and slightly tangy flavor complements sauces, stews, and other meals.

Violet Jasper

Main parameters
Fruit Color: **Purplish red with green stripes;** Germination: **7 to 21;** Maturity: **78;**
Determinate or indeterminate: **Indeterminate;**
Hybrid / Open Pollinated: **Open Pollinated**

Description
A one-of-a-kind Chinese cultivar. Hristo Hristov of Bulgaria first presented Tzi Bi U in the Seed Savers 2009 Yearbook. The seeds grow into enormous, robust, regular leaf plants that produce clusters of jewel-like, smooth, purplish-red tomatoes with iridescent green streaks and dark-purple red flesh. Fruit begins with deeper green stripes on normal unripe tomato green, and as the flesh darkens, the dark green stripes become somewhat opalescent. This one-of-a-kind cultivar appeals to me more for its decorative value than for its taste. These tomato seeds that are extremely rare [23].

Black Krim

Main parameters
Fruit Color: **Dark red-purple;** Germination: **7 to 14;** Maturity: **70-90;**
Determinate or indeterminate: **Indeterminate;**
Hybrid / Open Pollinated: **Open Pollinated**

Description
Also known as Black Crimea, Lars Olov Rosenstrom of Sweden introduced it to SSE. Originally from the Black Sea peninsula of Crimea. Beefsteak fruits are an unusual blend of violet-brown and purple-red—with enough sunshine and heat, they turn virtually black.

One of the greatest in terms of rich sweet taste. It consistently ranks well in tomato taste tests. It's really juicy. An heirloom from with enormous fruit, the delicious taste is prevalent in many West Coast markets and is a favorite of many good chefs.

Costoluto Florentino

Main parameters
Fruit Color: **Red;** Germination: **7 to 21;** Maturity: **80;**
Determinate or indeterminate: **Indeterminate;**
Hybrid / Open Pollinated: **Open Pollinated**

Description
The term costoluto refers to the flattened, strongly ribbed form of several Italian heirlooms. This lovely variety hails from Florence and wowed us with its early maturity of vivid crimson. Fruit is luscious and tasty when sliced, but it shines when slow-roasted or reduced into a rich sauce. In both hot and mild regions, indeterminate plants thrive.

This variety is well-suited for both fresh eating and cooking. Its sweet and juicy flavor is a great addition to salads, sandwiches, and snacks, and it also makes a great ingredient in sauces, stews, and other dishes.

Chocorella

Main parameters
Fruit Color: **Chocolate brown-red;** Germination: **7 to 21;**
Maturity: 75;
Determinate or indeterminate: **Indeterminate;**
Hybrid / Open Pollinated: **Open Pollinated**

Description
Chocorella is an heirloom tomato recognized for its distinctive chocolate-brown color and great flavor. This tomato ranges in size from medium to large and has a spherical to slightly flattened form.
The Chocorella tomato has a rich, dark brown skin with a somewhat rough texture. The flesh is juicy, sweet, and tasty, with a faint tanginess to it.
This type is suitable for both raw and cooked consumption. Its distinct flavor profile complements salads, sandwiches, and snacks, and it also works well in sauces, stews, and other foods.

Franchi Red Pear

Main parameters
Fruit Color: **Red;** Germination: **7 to 21;** Maturity: **85;**
Determinate or indeterminate: **Indeterminate;**
Hybrid / Open Pollinated: **Open Pollinated**

Description
Franchi is probably the world's oldest family business dealing with seeds. Its history goes back to 1783 - the year when the Montgolfier brothers took off in Paris for the first time with their hot air balloon, and when Mozart wrote his first oratorio. 220 years of experience in cultivation and breeding are reflected in each Franchi Sementi product.

This tomato is an excellent quality, flavorful, pear-shaped with vertical ribs - a must-try. Really meaty with minimal seeds.

Santorini

Main parameters
Fruit Color: **Red;** Germination: 5 **to 10;** Maturity: **80;**
Determinate or indeterminate: **Indeterminate;**
Hybrid / Open Pollinated: **Open Pollinated**

Description
Regular tomatoes don't usually have an interesting backstory, but the Santorini tomato does. It all began in 1917, when the Russian Revolution forced the closure of the majority of the country's Orthodox churches. At the time, the Greek volcanic island of Santorini was confronted with a new dilemma. Russian churches were their main customers for the wine manufactured by Greek Santorini monks. Recognizing the need for a new cash crop, the merchants resorted to an unexpected source: the Santorini tomato, which proved to be a profitable endeavor.

In 1818, a Capuchin monastery abbot imported cherry tomatoes to the Greek island. By the early 1900s, Santorini, Greece, had more than 20,000 acres of tomatoes under cultivation. The Santorini tomato has had an official designation of origin and has been protected since 2013.

These cherry tomatoes are tiny, with spherical, flat fruit produced by the plants. Santorini's hue is constantly rich red.

According to experts, Santorini cherry tomatoes are the world's richest tomato in lycopene, which gives the tomatoes their particular flavor [24].

Definitions

Determinate Tomatoes

A determinate tomato plant grows to a specific size and produces all of its fruit in a relatively short period of time. Determinate tomatoes are bushy and compact, making them ideal for growing in containers or small gardens.

One of the most distinguishing characteristics of determinate tomatoes is their consistent growth pattern. They reach a certain height, and then stop growing. They also produce all of their fruit at once, making them ideal for preserving and canning, as well as commercial agriculture.

Indeterminate Tomatoes

Indeterminate tomatoes are tomato plants that continue to grow and bear fruit throughout the growing season. Indeterminate tomatoes are more sprawling and take up more space to grow, but they produce fruit for a longer period of time.

Open-pollinated Tomatoes

Open-pollinated tomatoes are tomato plants that are developed from seeds produced through natural pollination rather than hybrid or genetically engineered seeds. Open-pollinated seeds can be preserved and replanted year after year, and the plants that develop from them produce fruit that is identical to the parent plant in look, growth habit, and flavor.

One of the primary benefits of open-pollinated tomatoes is that they are frequently well-suited to local growing circumstances. This is because open-pollination allows plants to change and adapt to their individual environment over time. This can result in plants that are stronger, more disease-resistant, and better adapted to the local growth circumstances.

Another advantage of open-pollinated tomatoes is that they frequently have a rich, nuanced flavor that gardeners and home cooks like. This is due to the fact that open-pollination permits the plant to establish its own distinct flavor character rather than depending on the uniform flavor of hybrid cultivars.

Hybrid Tomatoes

Hybrid tomatoes are a type of tomato plant that is created by cross-pollinating two different tomato species. These plants' offspring, known as hybrid seeds, will grow plants with qualities from both parent plants, such as size, shape, color, and flavor.

One of the primary benefits of hybrid tomatoes is that their growth habits, fruit output, and disease resistance are frequently more uniform and predictable. As a result, they are well-suited to commercial agriculture, where consistency and high yields are critical.

Another benefit of hybrid tomatoes is that they frequently have better disease resistance as well as resilience to environmental stresses like as heat, cold, and drought.

Heirloom Tomatoes

Heirloom tomatoes are tomato plants that have been passed down through multiple generations of a family and are regarded as an essential component of our agricultural legacy. Heirloom tomatoes are normally open-pollinated, which means they are grown from seeds produced by natural pollination rather than hybridization.

One of the most appealing aspects of heirloom tomatoes is their wide diversity of tastes, colors, and forms. In contrast to hybrid tomatoes, which are developed for uniformity and large yields, heirloom tomatoes are valued for their individual flavor characteristics, as well as their uncommon colors and forms.

Further Reading

I also read several gardening and tomato growing books. Some of my favorite tomato books are:

- Epic Tomatoes [25] by Craig LeHoullier is a gift and it won't disappoint you! For a new gardener, this book is the perfect resource to get inspired and learn the techniques needed. Even for me, as a gardener with a couple of years' experience, the book contained new information and beautiful photos that reignited my imagination and joy for the coming season.
- Tomato Container Gardening: 7 Easy Steps to Healthy Harvests from Small Spaces [26] by Mary Verdant comprehensively covering how to grow your tomatoes on a very small space. Mary proves that anyone, nearly anywhere can grow fresh tomatoes off the vine!
- Ten Tomatoes that Changed the World: A History [27] by William Alexander is a true fabulous read for any gardening nerd. If you love tomatoes or just history, you'll definitely like this book. Here you can learn how the tomato became something gourmet and loved.

Some notable others: Tomato: 80 Recipes Celebrating the Extraordinary Tomato [28], The Heirloom Tomato: From Garden to

Table: Recipes, Portraits, and History of the World's Most Beautiful Fruit [29] or the Tomato Grower's Answer Book [30].

References

[1] L. Bieri, "Pixabay - Fall, Old Man, Memories, Tomatoes," 2017. https://pixabay.com/photos/fall-old-man-memories-tomatoes-2099059/ (accessed Feb. 11, 2023).

[2] "Keeping Tomatoes Healthy in Hot Weather | Growing Franklin," 2019. https://u.osu.edu/growingfranklin/2019/07/16/keeping-tomatoes-healthy-in-hot-weather/comment-page-1/ (accessed Feb. 05, 2023).

[3] Tomato Dirt, "Shading Tomatoes: Reduce Their Stress, Keep Them Going in the Heat," *Tomato Dirt*. http://www.tomatodirt.com/shading-tomatoes.html (accessed Feb. 05, 2023).

[4] Bountiful Gardener, "Will Tomatoes Grow in Shade? – Bountiful Gardener," 2023. https://www.bountifulgardener.com/will-tomatoes-grow-in-shade/ (accessed Feb. 05, 2023).

[5] "Best Tomatoes For Shade – Learn About Shade Tolerant Tomato Varieties," *Gardening Know How*. https://www.gardeningknowhow.com/edible/

vegetables/tomato/growing-tomatoes-in-shade.htm (accessed Jan. 19, 2023).

[6] "Is a Tomato a Fruit or a Vegetable and Why?," 2020. https://www.eufic.org/en/healthy-living/article/is-a-tomato-a-fruit-or-a-vegetable-and-why (accessed Feb. 11, 2023).

[7] J. A. T. Pennington and R. A. Fisher, "Classification of fruits and vegetables," *Journal of Food Composition and Analysis*, vol. 22, pp. S23–S31, Dec. 2009, doi: 10.1016/j.jfca.2008.11.012.

[8] Pomidorlandia, "Tomatoes, Peppers, Seeds - Pomidorlandia.pl," 2023. https://pomidorlandia.pl/en/ (accessed Feb. 11, 2023).

[9] Totally Tomatoes, "Totally Tomatoes: Tomatoes, Peppers, Vegetables & More," 2023. https://www.totallytomato.com/ (accessed Feb. 11, 2023).

[10] Jung Seed, "Jung Seed: Vegetable Seed, Flower Seed, and Garden Supplies," 2023. https://www.jungseed.com/ (accessed Feb. 11, 2023).

[11] Baker Creek, "Rare Heirloom Seeds| Baker Creek Heirloom Seeds," 2023. https://www.rareseeds.com/ (accessed Feb. 11, 2023).

[12] J. Chan, "T&T Seeds," *T&T Seeds*, 2023. https://ttseeds.com/ (accessed Feb. 11, 2023).

[13] "Paradicsomtermesztő csoport | Facebook," 2023. https://www.facebook.com/groups/ 1617961958523992 (accessed Feb. 11, 2023).

[14] "How Volcanic Soil Gives Us Tomatoes Primed For Neapolitan Pizza Glory," *Atlas Obscura.* https://www.atlasobscura.com/foods/ san-marzano-tomatoes (accessed Jan. 30, 2023).

[15] "Isis Candy Cherry Tomato," *Seed Savers Exchange.* https://www.seedsavers.org/isis-candy-tomato (accessed Jan. 28, 2023).

[16] "Isis Candy Cherry Tomato," Nov. 13, 2022. https://www.rareseeds.com/isis-candy-cherry-tomato (accessed Jan. 28, 2023).

[17] A. R, "17 Unique Tomato Varieties That Grow In Shade," *KitchenCuddle,* 2023. https://kitchencuddle.com/tomato-varieties-that-grow-in-shade/ (accessed Feb. 11, 2023).

[18] Tomato Growers Supply Company, "Mama Leone Tomato," *Tomato Growers Supply Company*, 2023. https://tomatogrowers.com/products/mama-leone (accessed Feb. 11, 2023).

[19] Pomidorlandia, "Belize Pink Heart - Seeds: Tomatoes Tomatoes, Peppers, Seeds - Pomidorlandia.pl," 2023. https://pomidorlandia.pl/en/produkt/2360/ belize-pink-heart (accessed Feb. 11, 2023).

[20] White Flower Farm, "Tomato 'Carmello,'" *White Flower Farm*, 2023. https://www.whiteflowerfarm.com/4860-product.html (accessed Feb. 11, 2023).

[21] Territorial Seed, "Carmello Tomato Seed," *Territorial Seed*, 2023. https://territorialseed.com/products/tomato-carmello (accessed Feb. 11, 2023).

[22] Victory Seed Company, "Siberia Tomato - Heirloom, Open-Pollinated, non-Hybrid Victory Seeds®," *Victory Seed Company*, 2023. https://victoryseeds.com/products/siberia-tomato (accessed Feb. 11, 2023).

[23] TomatoFest, "Violet Jasper Organic Tomato Seeds | TomatoFest," *www.tomatofest.com*, 2023. https://www.tomatofest.com/product_p/tf-0513e1.htm (accessed Feb. 11, 2023).

[24] A. Bree, "The Santorini Tomato - Minneopa Orchards," Apr. 19, 2022. https://minnetonkaorchards.com/santorini-tomato/ (accessed Feb. 11, 2023).

[25] C. LeHoullier, *Epic tomatoes: how to select & grow the best varieties of all time*. North Adams, MA: Storey Publishing, 2015.

[26] M. Verdant, *Tomato Container Gardening: 7 Easy Steps To Healthy Harvests from Small Spaces*. 2012.

[27] W. Alexander, *Ten tomatoes that changed the world: a history*, First edition. New York: Grand Central Publishing, 2022.

[28] C. Thomson, *Tomato: 80 recipes celebrating the extraordinary tomato*. London: Quadrille, an imprint of Hardie Grant Publishing, 2022.

[29] A. Goldman and V. Schrager, *The heirloom tomato: from garden to table: recipes, portraits, and history of the world's most beautiful fruit*, 1st U.S. ed. New York: Bloomsbury: Distributed to the trade by Macmillan, 2008.

[30] S. Albert, *Tomato grower's answer book*. Kenwood, CA: Green Wagon Books, 2019.